Rising
Above
Opioid
Addiction

An Indigenous Woman's Story of
Childhood Trauma, Faith & Healing

Foreword by DONNA PARTOW

SIERA TAKETCHERA RUSSELL

DEDICATION

To my daughter and granddaughter, to all our relations, and to all our descendants to come…

ACKNOWLEDGMENTS

Jesus Christ, my beloved Lord: Thank You for loving me and being my best friend since I was six years old. My heart overflows with gratitude. What an exciting life You have given me!

Aaron (Yavapai), my late dad: Thank you for loving God, loving me, and demonstrating a life of faith and courage.

Maureen Kane, Esq.: Your legal, editing, and writing skills assisted me in completing my manuscript. You are a lovely human being with tremendous patience, compassion, and kindness. We did it, Mo!

Donna Partow: God's favor and anointing on your life has profoundly impacted my destiny. You inspire and mentor me to rise above mediocrity and live a purposeful, God-centered life. Your teachings are priceless and have guided me in writing my story.

Professor Rebecca Tsosie (Yaqui): Words fail to express my deep gratitude for your countless contributions to Indigenous communities and peoples across the world. Thank you for your valued friendship, insight, and encouragement to complete my manuscript.

Sunny Lehman (Odawa): Without fail, you extended your hand of friendship during my loneliest times. Without judgment, you answered my calls and graciously connected me with a community of loving believers.

Lura (Kiowa) and your late husband, Ron Olander (Ojibwe), Soaring Eagles Native Ministries Founders: Your energetic passion and commitment for discipling Indigenous peoples have comforted and inspired me.

Darlene Jenks, spiritual mom and former president of West Valley Aglow: You have showered me with courage and love. Your support helped me acclimate back into society and paved the way for this book.

Chaplain Linda Hudgins: You have been a role model and treasured friend during my transition from disabled to abled. You brought laughter and security into my life.

Debby Brawner, friend and author: You showed unconditional love and friendship, and your publishing accomplishment inspired me to finish my story.

Rev. Bill (Yaqui) and Jan Gowey: Your love and involvement in my parents' lives during their golden years spoke volumes about God's love. You exemplify God's love in action.

Dr. Ruth Ann Marston: You believed in my unique skills and abilities when I did not. You are an inspiration and trusted advisor.

Professor Mary Dolores Guerra: You opened the door to your classroom so that I could observe a new way of teaching law. Your kindness on that one day opened a new career for me. You are an amazing mentor and friend.

Judge Kyle and Annie Fields: You held me accountable for completing my manuscript. Our friendship is a great source of joy.

Louise Sandoval: You celebrated my achievements, shared in my disappointments, and encouraged my book completion. You're a trooper and a beloved friend.

Sacheen, my daughter and author: Your support and compassion for my story is priceless! My heart is filled with love for you and GG.

CONTENTS

A SPECIAL GIFT FOR YOU

Hunigum:

That's my way of saying "Thank You" in Yavapai.

I'm so honored you've decided to buy my book and travel along my path for a short while. I pray your heart will be touched.

As you'll soon discover, one thing that made a difference in my life were wise mentors. If you want help to achieve your dreams—then I invite you to grab a copy of my free guide, "***Powerful Questions Every Mentor Should Ask***."

Just go to WWW.INDIGENOUSMENTORS.COM.

Along with my free gift, I offer biblical principles to encourage women to walk in beauty and live their best life ever. If you are a woman seeking opportunities to prosper, join my Facebook group: Indigenous Mentors - Connecting Indigenous Women Making A Difference.

You can find the group here:
HTTPS://WWW.FACEBOOK.COM/GROUPS/INDIGENOUSMENTORS.

N'ach gavavie ngum.

That's my way of saying "I will keep you in my prayers" in Yavapai.

Siera Taketchera Russell

FOREWORD

I couldn't believe it.

No one would believe it.

This beautiful, brilliant, Harvard-educated indigenous leader was telling me she'd been a suicidal opioid addict. Not only before … but even after her rise through the most elite of America's educational institutions.

How was this possible? Words like *appellate judge* and a*ddict* don't seem to belong in the same sentence.

How did she descend into such utter darkness … and how did she ever find her way out again? Those were the questions racing through my mind when I urged Siera to write this book. Not for herself. But for the millions of people affected by the addiction crisis gripping the planet in this hour.

If she can become ensnared, it can happen to anyone. And it is happening. Among the rich and the poor. Among the young and the old. It's reaching into every level of society. First, it happened to *them*. People we found easy to dismiss. But now it's happening to *us*. We cannot continue to ignore this crisis.

In this brave memoir of trauma and triumph, what impressed me most is Siera's complete lack of guile. She lays it all on the table: equally as straightforward about her gifts and strengths as she is about her weaknesses and failures. Both are part of her story. Just as both are part of every addict's story.

On these pages, we meet a real person. Just like the real people all around you who are struggling against addiction. Maybe even people you love. Or someone you look at in the mirror every morning.

Her goal in writing, and my dream as I heartily endorse this book, is to show the way forward through faith, hope, and love.

When Siera sent me the final manuscript, I literally couldn't put it down. I suspect you'll have the same reaction. I closed the book with renewed faith in God and a fresh determination to believe that there really is a hope and a future for everyone, including those swept up into today's drug epidemic. Because with God, all things are still possible.

Donna Partow,
Bestselling author, *Becoming the Woman God Wants Me To Be*

INTRODUCTION

Opioid addiction has become a national nightmare. No one is spared—no ethnic group, no income level, neither young nor old. No one sets out to be an addict. It happens little by little, choice by choice.

I have lived it myself, as a Native American Indigenous woman who plunged from the lofty heights of Harvard to the dehumanizing depths of institutionalized detox.

After my recovery, I served as an associate judge in a rural tribal court in the Southwestern United States. As a judge, I saw many people who had made bad decisions and had to live with the consequences. And occasionally I found myself thinking, "There, but for the grace of God, go I." I saw much suffering, much sorrow, and sometimes, much relief.

Addicts are people who hurt—who need to feel loved and accepted, not rejected and scorned. I am one who found freedom in the promise that there is nothing impossible for God. "With man this is impossible, but not with God; all things are possible with God" (Mark 10:27 NIV).

In this narrative of my own life decisions, suffering, and redemption, I hope to inspire others to never give up, to nurture our children, to be compassionate with those who suffer, and, above all, to trust in God.

Chapter One
TRIBAL JUSTICE

*Hear the disputes between your people
and judge fairly.
Deuteronomy 1:16 (NIV)*

On a cool Wednesday evening, in the mountains shadowing the valley's river, a hurting young Native man committed suicide. Within forty-eight hours, repercussions of this tragedy came before me as the presiding judge in our community court. At approximately 4:30 p.m. on Friday, the deceased's father filed for an emergency injunction, asking the court to stop the burial that his son's estranged wife had set for sunrise the next day. In chambers, I reviewed the father's petition and prepared for the hearing.

As the clerk of the court announced, "All rise, the Honorable Judge presiding," I walked to my seat.

"Thank you. Please be seated," I said as I faced the father and his family members, and silently prayed to Creator God for wisdom.

The father was a man in his fifties, maybe older. He stood at the petitioner's table on the right side of the courtroom. A young man and woman stood a few rows behind him. Probably in their late teens or early twenties, the two strongly resembled the father.

I asked the father to state his name for the record. As he spoke, I studied his appearance. Although tall and strong in stature, his face was woefully fatigued.

"Your Honor," he began, "I am a member of this tribe. I am the father of the deceased." He said that the young man and woman with him in the courtroom were also his children—the deceased's brother and sister.

The family's Native American heritage was obvious, and so was their heartache. I felt the young people's eyes focus on me as I listened to their father's testimony.

"Your Honor, the estranged wife is preparing a Hopi burial for my son, because she claims that my son adopted the Hopi way—her way. Judge, you can't let her do that."

Although my heart ached for this family, I listened dispassionately as the father continued. "This woman planned a Hopi burial to take place at sunrise tomorrow morning, just three days after my son's death."

The wife was not at this hearing, so I couldn't question her. But I had no reason to doubt the father was telling the truth. "Your Honor, this woman and my son weren't even living together! They've been estranged for some time now. And my son has been living at his aunt's house, not with his wife."

The father also testified that the wife was refusing to allow him or his son's mother to attend the burial. "His mother, she's a Lakota Sioux. She has to drive a thousand miles to get here. She won't arrive until Saturday afternoon. So even if this woman lets us attend the Hopi burial, his mother won't get here in time for the ceremony because it's scheduled for sunrise."

I continued to listen objectively, even though my heart went out to the father and his children. The family's anguish was compounded because the son had committed suicide; his death was unnatural and unexpected.

The father persisted. "Your Honor, please, please. My wife and I and our children need to say goodbye to our son and brother. We need to give him a Christian burial. Please help us, Judge. We're begging you."

Throughout their father's testimony, the brother and sister listened, nodding their heads while holding back emotion. Harm to this family seemed inevitable if I were to allow that burial to proceed as planned. My decision needed to protect the sanctity of this family.

I had experience with Christian funerals in our tribal community, but I knew nothing about Hopi burial customs. The deceased had died intestate—without a will—and his father, mother, and siblings wanted to bury their beloved son and brother in the Christian tradition on our reservation. But the estranged wife's Hopi burial plans excluded members of his immediate family. I presumed that a Hopi burial meant that his body would be buried several hundred miles away. My heart pounded as I realized the impact my decision would have on this family and the wife's family.

With a mixture of sorrow and anger, the father reiterated his and his family's love for the deceased, their need to say good-bye, and the need to have a Christian burial with a tribal pastor. "This woman does not have the right to keep us away from our son, the boy we raised," he said. The brother and sister continued nodding with wet eyes and anguished faces as their father begged me to grant the emergency injunction to stop the Hopi burial and allow a Christian funeral to move forward.

Then the father stated emphatically, "My son is not a Hopi, Your Honor. He is one of us!"

After hearing the testimony, I granted the injunction to prevent the estranged wife from burying the deceased at dawn the next day. As I pronounced the decision, the father's face reflected relief and, for a moment, joy. His children looked relieved as well. I can still hear the father's weary voice repeating, "Thank you, thank you," as the clerk called, "All rise," and I headed into my chambers.

Alone in chambers, I felt some relief and peace. The heaviness seemed to have lifted. With the hearing concluded, I now had to write the order of injunction.

It was now past normal business hours; 5:00 p.m. had come and gone. The clerk and I were the only remaining court personnel. The clerk told the family they could go home; a tribal police officer would personally serve the court order on the wife and the father as soon as I had completed it. The family left, and the officer waited for my order.

Shortly after the family left, the clerk came into my office. "Judge," she said, "I just want you to know that the tribal police will be out there in the morning to maintain the peace. Things might get out of hand when the wife tries to go ahead with the burial at sunrise." The clerk continued to explain that a community protest was expected. The clerk said she had heard that the wife and her family had gotten wind of the injunction and were still planning to hold the Hopi burial ceremony. "And part of it will take place in our gym right across the street!"

I was mortified. "What! I thought the Hopi burial would take place on the Hopi reservation, a good distance away from our community!" Shocked, I directed the clerk to locate the wife and notify her and the father that they would both need to appear at another hearing that evening. The injunction had not been issued.

Now keeping the peace was paramount. Determined to avoid a potential community brawl, I focused my attention on gaining a better understanding of the legal and cultural rights and duties of the respective parties.

Several questions stirred in my thoughts: Who had the legal rights to the deceased's remains— his Apache and Sioux parents or his Hopi wife? Is there a property right in human bones, that is, does someone own them? Had the deceased man adopted the Hopi way of life, or would he have wanted a Christian burial? What tribal or state law or tribal custom or tradition gives the parents the right to bury their son if he was married but living apart from his wife?

Similarly, these questions applied to the wife's desire to exclude the deceased's parents and siblings from her late husband's burial ceremony. Could I lawfully or ethically delay a burial if doing so would breach a sacred rite? And could I base my decision on what felt like the right and compassionate thing to do, even if the law directed otherwise?

As I mulled over these questions and the effect their answers would have on my decision, it occurred to me that two years earlier, I had been dangerously close to the desperation this man must have felt before he ended his own life. Now the deceased would make no more decisions on this earth. He had seen no other way out from his pain; this young Native man had succumbed to the darkness.

I saw the havoc his suicide had wreaked on his family members and his community. Grief shrouded the father and siblings when they gathered in my courtroom. I felt grateful that I had risen up out of my many dark valleys and had not committed suicide. I was still alive. And I still had decisions to make.

Despite my feeling blessed and grateful, gone was the sense of relief I had felt moments earlier, when I thought this matter had been resolved. I dialed the number of a mentor, a well-respected Hopi tribal court judge. I anxiously prayed he would answer his phone and clarify some cultural questions. And again and more fervently—and not for the first time—I prayed to Creator God for wisdom.

Chapter Two

ABANDONED

Before I formed you in the womb, I knew you;
before you were born, I set you apart.
Jeremiah 1:5 (NIV)

I remember the first time I desperately prayed to God. I wanted something far more tangible than wisdom then. I needed an escape. My mom certainly was going to kill me, literally. She was viciously beating me—I thought I'd die. I was seven years old. If only God would stop her—if only my "real" mom would rescue me.

My mother, the woman who raised me, wasn't my "real" mom—although she eventually adopted me. I hadn't quite turned one month old when my biological mother, living in a ghetto neighborhood in California, decided she could not keep me. So she passed me to her brother, my biological uncle, and his emotionally wounded wife, determining my fate but not sealing it.

Raised on a reservation in the Southwest, my birth mom grew up with eight siblings. She spoke her native language at home and learned English at school. Her father, my grandpa, provided for his large family on a modest income. My grandpa and grandma were of the same tribe and they both became Christians in the 1920s. All of their children were full-blooded American Indians.

My birth mom grew into a tall and attractive young lady, with ebony hair and eyes to match. She loved to laugh, dance, and draw attention. She was a vibrant teenager in the 1940s and a stunning young woman in the 50s.

During the 1950s, Congress authorized funds for a relocation program as part of the US government's vacillating federal policy toward the American Indian tribes. This federal relocation program arose during an era known in federal and tribal historical relations as the Termination Era.

Numerous tribes had their federal trust relationship terminated during this era. Congress had intended to eliminate the federal government's fiduciary responsibility to Indian tribes as established under federal law and treaties. Government officials distributed flyers across Indian Country enticing American Indians to leave their reservations and attend urban vocational training and education programs. Congress wanted American Indians to assimilate into the general population and, in doing so, relieve Congress of its duty to provide health care, education services, and overall tribal government development.

As a result of the relocation program, thousands of American Indians left their reservations and relocated to destination cities, including San Francisco, Cleveland, Denver, Dallas, Minneapolis, St. Louis, Salt Lake City, Seattle, Oklahoma City, Chicago, Houston, and Los Angeles. The government promised stipends to cover housing, living, and education costs in these relocation cities. It was another broken promise that sparked the evolution of urban American Indian ghettos.

For many young American Indians in the Southwest, leaving the confines of the reservation to chase the promise of a better life in California proved too inviting an adventure to pass up. My birth mom and six of her siblings also relocated.

Sadly, after a few months in the big city, my birth mom found herself pregnant and not married, a huge transgression for a single woman in the 1950s, and much more so for a Native woman. She gave birth to a healthy baby girl—me. She mothered me for a few weeks, then she handed me to her brother and his wife. I was never returned.

Less than twelve years later, at the age of thirty-three, she would violently die at the hands of her boyfriend when she was eight months pregnant. My unborn sibling perished also. I was eleven years old when they passed. God only knows what her life would have been like had she stayed on the reservation, but that was not my birth mom's choice or her destiny.

Chapter Three
LOST CHILDHOOD

*The Lord is close to the brokenhearted
and saves those who are crushed in spirit.*
Psalm 34:18 (NIV)

The 1955 summer in Los Angeles was hot and humid as usual. That oppressive heat and the absence of air conditioning may have contributed to my adoptive mother's growing resentment towards me, a needy infant. I can speculate and make excuses for her, but the truth is, I will never understand—and nothing justifies—the extent of her hostility toward me right from the start. The woman I called my mother, the woman who raised me, had a sickness, a deep, dark anger that targeted me from my earliest memories.

My adoptive mother chronically abused me in all areas of my development. From the time they adopted me until I turned six, my adoptive father was often gone in the evenings. I don't know what he did, but he wasn't home to protect me. My mother terrorized me when my dad wasn't home.

From around age four through fourteen, I felt intense feelings of abandonment, fear, and worthlessness. My mother's abuse, combined with my father's absences, resulted in memories that resemble nightmares more than real life. The only nonabusive memories I recall from those childhood years involve experiences at school, at church, and with extended family.

Memories of times when my mother was playful or loving toward me are tragically limited. It didn't take much to set my mother into a rage. Instead, she routinely abused me, but the physical punches wounded me less deeply than the profound and devastating emotional gashes.

I remember too many examples of abuse to list, but a few instances are important to share. These situations help provide an understanding of how, with God's help, an abused child can live a productive, quality adult life rather than repeat violent, shaming acts against his or her children. Even now, after some six decades, it's extremely painful to remember the vulnerable little girl I was.

Some four-year-olds like exploring or chasing and catching bugs, but I was not one of them. I was terrified of bugs, and my mother knew it. If she became enraged or moody, she would shove me out the back door of our tiny one-bedroom apartment onto the cement stairs and into the back yard. The yard was overgrown with dying grass, weeds, and stickers—an uncared for patch of land, small and fenced in. Just beyond the yard were the railroad tracks. There was no one nearby—no children to play with—no one to hear my screams.

I would sit on the top of the concrete stairs, trying to stay out of the prickly, bug-infested grass. With one arm, I cradled my knees to my chest to try to deflect the many flying insects and hopping grasshoppers that surrounded me. With my other hand, I reached up and shook the screen-door handle as I begged my mother to let me in, even though I knew that a beating with her fist, or any object she could get her hands on, awaited me once I crawled inside.

My mother knew I was terrified. And she just let me scream—scream and plead—to no avail. Eventually, she would unlock the screen door and, seething with disgust at my pained face, shame me for it.

"Stop crying, you stupid, filthy girl or I'll give you something to cry about!" Her vicious words rang in my ears, as her hands slapped and punched my face, arms, and any exposed skin. She'd shove my face onto the floor. I'd curl into a ball with my arms crossed behind my head. As her blows struck my head, I tried to hide my face and pressed it hard into the concrete. And each time I was assaulted on that day and the hundreds of days after, I mentally disappeared in order to survive the excruciating ordeal.

Not too long after living near the train tracks, we moved to another suburb in the Los Angeles area. One day, my mother and I had taken the bus into downtown Los Angeles from Inglewood. I was about five years old and very excited to ride on the bus. On the return trip, the bus stopped, we stepped off, and I began to run across the empty graveled lot toward our apartment.

But then I stumbled. My hands scraped across the ground as I slid forward. A small, sharp rock became embedded in the palm of my hand. It hurt and I cried in pain.

But no comfort or compassion came from my mother. She grabbed my arm and dragged me across the lot and through our apartment door, all the while shouting shaming insults at me. "You got what you deserved, you stupid, ugly girl." Then indoors, the painful, torturous rituals began again.

It was during my kindergarten year that my mother began the bedtime abuse. "Go to bed now, and when I come back, you'd better be asleep!" she'd yell. I tried so hard to go to sleep, but most nights I just couldn't because I feared her return. To catch me not asleep, she would pull back the blanket I had tried to cower under. Or she'd turn the light on to see if my eyelids moved. If she saw any eye movement, she would punch my body, yank me by the hair out of bed, and call me degrading names.

This torment would be repeated over and over at night whenever my father was gone. And for the first decade of my life, it seemed like he was almost always gone when my mother said it was my bedtime.

I dreaded bedtime and agonized every night, always afraid she'd come into my room and beat me with her hairbrush or a hanger and drag me across the floor. The wire hanger had become one of her favorite weapons. I would desperately try to crawl under the bed. But I was never able to escape.

"Go to sleep! You stupid, dirty girl!" she would yell while pelting me. She would hold the weapon in one hand and try to pry my arms from around my head with the other. I did my best to protect my face by burying my head between my arms with my little hands grasping the back of my neck. By the time she tired of repeating this horrific scene each night, I mentally went away—disassociated from the experience—only to face another day and another ritualistic bedtime torture.

On one unusual night when I was five, my mother took me with her to visit a neighbor's apartment. When this neighbor opened her door, I saw a smiling lady standing in a brightly lit, colorful space with an amazing collection of knickknacks. Positioned on one shelf stood a beautiful American Indian ceramic doll. I was drawn to its clothing and brown-colored skin. Unfortunately, my mouth spoke before I could stop myself. I committed an unthinkable act in my mother's presence. I pointed to the doll and said out loud, "I like that!"

Fear welled up when I caught my mother's eyes. I'd awakened the "shadow monster." Unaware of the looming consequences, the kind lady handed me the doll and said, "Here, take it!" I was surprised by this unfamiliar kindness. Then the shadow monster spoke. "No, she can't have that. I'm sorry for what she's done."

My hand was crushed in the monster's hand as she dragged me outside and up the stairs to our apartment. Terror gripped my little heart almost as painfully as her hand gripped mine. Inside our kitchen, she forced my clenched hand over a heated electric burner then shoved me into the bathroom. She turned the faucet on full blast and the tub quickly filled. Her silence terrorized me as much as when she physically and verbally assaulted me. She ordered me to take my clothes off. I was so very scared she would hurt me until I died, and then my "real" mother would never find me.

My mother shoved my panties into my face and rubbed them viciously back and forth. She screamed horrible things as I climbed into the tub. "You're so dirty. You're a dirty, filthy little girl! Nobody likes a dirty girl!"

Trying to obey in the best way I could, I sat with my legs stretched out toward the spigot and my back straight. She didn't want me to lean back. I focused on my toes poking out of the water. They pointed to the ceiling. They wanted to wiggle.

But I couldn't move. Movement meant a slap or a punch or having my hair viciously yanked. We sat in the bathroom for an eternity, the shadow monster and I. The monster forced me to stay frozen. I sat in the water, facing forward, eyes open, paralyzed with fear and painfully rigid. I ignored the cramping in my back and legs. Maybe it wasn't as bad as her punches would be if I dared move.

Eventually, she allowed me out of the tub. But the bedroom torture was next. My childhood nightmares happened before I fell asleep, not after.

These repeated incidents of abuse happened all too often. The little girl who I was knew no other way of being, no other source of love or affection, no tenderness or acceptance.

Chapter Four
BEST FRIEND

Jesus said, "Let the little children come to me, and do not hinder them, for the kingdom of heaven belongs to such as these."
Matthew 19:14 (NIV)

A glimmer of hope arrived the summer I turned six. My family moved from California to a rural town in my dad's home state. When I was in class, I felt valued. With school over, I was worried. What would I do? Where could I go to stay safe? But God had a solution. He led me to another safe haven.

That summer, I was allowed to attend a vacation Bible school run by the First Baptist Church. Someone from the church had knocked at our door and invited my parents to enroll me in the school for the summer. The church was close to our home, and it became a refuge for me.

It was one of the hottest days on record. And I headed out to vacation Bible school. I devoured every word a Baptist preacher lovingly spoke about the Son of God, Jesus Christ. My curiosity peaked. My body grew warm and tingly the more I heard about Christ's love for me. It was the first time I heard that I was loved. My little-girl heart opened up to the Holy Spirit's gentle nudge. When the preacher asked if any of us children wanted to receive God's love, I was ready. With a child's pure heart, I grabbed on to the message of God's love and salvation, crying, "Yes, Jesus come into my heart!" In that moment, a supernatural miracle occurred. God transformed me from the daughter of my earthly parents to the daughter of the Living God. I was "born again" into the eternal family of God. From that moment on, Jesus became my best friend and has never left me.

I vividly remember a painting on the wall behind the baptismal pool in the church sanctuary. It portrayed a tranquil, perfect world, one with a beautiful aqua river running through soft green grass into infinity. In the intensely blue sky was a shining sun. I loved this painted scene and the serenity it depicted. It felt peaceful and inviting.

As I listened to the pastor share verses from the Bible—verses telling me that God loved me just as I was—I daydreamed myself into that painless world. It captivated my heart with feelings of love and belonging I had never known. No matter what happened to me at home, I knew in my heart I had a best friend, a friend God had sent because He so loved the world—and me.

Jesus became my dearest friend. His picture hung in our Sunday school classroom and I loved to see his soft and loving smile directed at me. I was so happy when I asked Him to come into my heart and life! From that moment on, He became my best friend and, at six years old, I didn't feel so alone anymore.

Even though I knew I had a friend who loved me, I continued to walk through my childhood years in constant fear of my mother. She was the only mother who raised me. I never knew when my mother would explode and attack me. My feelings of fear and worthlessness were reinforced by her rage and unpredictable torture. Even though I didn't always understand the words in her degrading barrage of insults, I believed that I was a bad girl who deserved to be scolded and physically punished.

Once when I was just shy of seven, my mother was beating me. I felt something in me shift. This attack would be different. Something in me sensed that I was not alone in the house with the shadow monster. Jesus, my Lord and Savior, my all-powerful best friend, was there too. As my mother punched me with her fists, I cried out for help as loud as my seven-year-old lungs could yell. "Help me! Jesus, please help me!"

But my mother's assault did not wane. And neither did God nor his Son nor his legions of angels come down from heaven to help me. "God doesn't help bad girls like you!" sneered my mother.

Her words took root in the depths of my soul. "Bad girl, bad, dirty girl! God doesn't help bad girls like you!" I was crushed. My hope was extinguished.

In those terrorizing moments, during the torrent of rage directed my way, my mother's statements certainly seemed true. I didn't understand why God allowed her to hurt me during those beatings and torrential downpours of mean words. My best friend, Jesus, had not come to my rescue. I had no other choice but to believe my mother's words—to believe the obvious reality of what I was experiencing by her hands. No powerful God or avenging angel had supernaturally appeared or would ever appear to strike her down and save me.

No, I was the only one stricken down—the bad, dirty girl. My circumstances reinforced this wrong belief. I didn't know anything other than what I endured almost daily, vulnerable and afraid, behind closed doors.

The shift was that I took hold of this ungodly belief and it defined my identity—the way I viewed myself. By age seven, the identity that would shape my decisions and my life for years to come had taken hold, like a poisonous vine wrapped around a rosebush, choking off light and life.

Chapter Five
FEAR AND FAITH

Whenever I was knocked down,
He reached down and saved me.
Psalm 116:6 (VOICE)

School was a safe place and esteem builder. In classrooms, I felt confident and accepted. I experienced joy and value when a teacher showed me approval. I'd regularly hear, "Good job, Siera!" or "That's right!" Approving comments watered my God-planted seed of hope. The accolades gave me a reason to keep doing what I did best— schoolwork. With each morsel of praise, I determined in my heart to do more and do better. I flourished in school. Academic excellence defined me from grade school through college.

Around the age of ten, my parents took me to attend our school's parent-teacher conference. This was a new experience and I felt anxious. I prayed and hoped that my dad would be proud of me.

It was early evening when we arrived at my school. Parents were crisscrossing the school yard, scurrying along the sidewalks, clutching papers and checking room numbers. They soon began disappearing inside open classroom doors. My parents followed suit, disappearing into my fifth grade teacher's classroom. With worried thoughts ricocheting in my head, I nervously waited for them outside.

What was my teacher going to tell them? Did I do something wrong today? What's going to happen? My pacing pressed my footsteps into the grass. An eternity later my parents emerged and walked toward me. I tried to figure out what they were thinking and quickly scanned their faces. I stepped toward them. My father's eyes locked on mine. His kind eyes flashed, his face smiled, and his words exploded. "Your teacher said you are smart!"

My chest lifted to catch my breath. I felt relieved and special. Dad said that I was smart. I felt like the most popular girl in class. Confident, admired, and beautiful. My heart gripped this experience like a struggling swimmer grabbing at a life raft. "You're smart!" was planted into the garden of my soul.

During fifth grade, I was included in our high school's band for a Christmas concert in the cafeteria. I played the clarinet and was thrilled to be invited. This would be my first performance in front of parents. On the evening of our concert, my father wasn't home and my mother said she wasn't going to attend. I got ready to walk back to school to be on time for our band's performance. Before I left, my mother told me to meet her at a school gate near the cafeteria immediately after the concert.

The cafeteria was crowded and the music was good. Then the concert ended. I packed my clarinet and moved quickly through the families. I hurried to the gate and looked for my mother. Fear gripped my chest and it was hard to breathe because I couldn't see her. Tall people with their kids started exiting and passing by. I instinctively began to race toward home fearing she had already come and left. I was afraid of being alone and left behind. I was panicked.

As I burst through the door of my parents' apartment, my eyes focused on my ten-year-old cousin sitting in front of the television. He had turned toward the sound of our rusty screen door swinging open. "Where is she?" I shouted, my voice quivered, and desperation darkened my face.

"She's gone to get you," he replied and turned back to his show. "Isn't she with you?"

I pivoted so fast that his question seemed to linger in the apartment without reaching my ears. But I had heard those dreaded words—isn't she with you?

Terror spread like the black plague throughout my body as I ran back to school. I prayed that my mother would not already be at the gate. I knew she would be horribly angry and hurt me for not being at the right spot. My thoughts frantically replayed the last moments with her, hoping to remember some forgotten instruction. I was in a crazed race through the side roads, returning to the school grounds. The shadow monster had assured me that, once the concert ended, I would find her waiting at the gate. Then we would both walk the distance back to my parents' apartment in the projects. She had not given directions for an early-ending concert. "Please God," I prayed, "don't let her be there before me."

Pushing past the crowd of concert leavers, I strained to catch sight of her. Panic gripped me and adrenaline surged. I was gasping due to fear and running. Finally, I reached the gate. Anxiety rose as my eyes scanned the groups of moving parents and children filing past me. I heard the praises and laughter. Street lamps illuminated the smiling faces and hugs. Public displays of affection were directed at the other child performers. The gaiety all around only emphasized my fear and loneliness.

"Super playing, young lady," a classmate's dad said to me as he walked by with his arm around his son. I did my best to say thank you in spite of the tightness in my throat. Bodies brushed past and off the school grounds. I grew increasingly more fearful as the crowd blended into the dark and disappeared. "Where is she?" I asked myself.

Abruptly my search ended. Walking toward me was the shadow monster. Terrified, I faced my mother on the emptying school property. My heartbeats began drowning out other sounds and I struggled to control my shaking. In silence, I screamed for a miracle. "Help me, Jesus!" My adrenaline surge kept me upright. I took the

stance of a warrior awaiting the battle cry, prepared to die.

Rage emanated from my mother. It seethed out of
her every pore. I easily and accurately sensed my
mother's mood. Everything about her demeanor
was painfully familiar. The moon's light revealed
her narrowed eyes, fierce face, and bared teeth.
She was a grizzly bear cornering its prey. Sadly, I
was more afraid of being left behind than enduring
whatever attack lay ahead.

"Where have you been, you stupid girl? I told you
to wait right there and again you don't listen!
You're disgusting and make me ashamed!" My in-
sides twisted into thorn-covered pretzels, slicing
my soul. These wounds ripped into my small
quantity of self-esteem as I was pelted with demeaning words.

The monster leaned into my face and continued
in a hateful yet lowered voice, "You bad, horrible
girl. Ugly, disgusting girl—can't you do anything
right? How dare you wander off when you were
told to wait right here!" Spit bullets bounced off
my frightened face. I dropped my head, stared at
the ground in an act of deference and pathetic

homage to my tyrannical mother. I silently prayed for help; it was all that I knew to do.

After what seemed an eternity, her verbal abuse stopped. My mother turned away from me and headed in the direction of the apartment. I started to follow behind her with head down and my chin close to my chest. I kept my eyes raised just enough to keep my mother's feet in sight and fought back the tears filling my eyes.

She had only taken a few steps when she stopped, whirled around, and yelled, "Where do you think you're going?" I stopped in sync with her movement, and softly responded, "Home."

While I froze under my mother's glare, the night's darkness intensified. Now the school grounds were emptied. The next words that shot out from my mother's mouth shattered my world.

"Do not follow me! Don't you dare come home! You don't have a home! Go away!" She turned her back on me and stormed off toward the projects. Shocked and terrified, I remained frozen, watching her backside disappear into the evening darkness. I was only ten years old, terrified of being left alone, and abandoned again by a parent.

Here, in the emptied school grounds, I was experiencing my greatest fear. What was I going to do? Where could I go? What is going to happen to me? What was so wrong with me? Even though my mother was cruel, her violence wasn't as frightening to my child's mind as was physical abandonment. My fear was almost paralyzing and I was also afraid of the dark.

The moonlight and a few lights on the school ground kept me from being in complete darkness when my mother walked away. After a few minutes, something inside me said to walk. Putting one foot in front of the other, I began moving toward the only safe place I had ever known. My feet headed down a dirt road toward the Baptist church. Most of the town's porch lights from the scattered homes were turned off but the moon's light helped me see the church steeple.

As I slowly walked toward the darkened church building, I began praying to God to help me. There wasn't anyone at the church because no lights were on. What was I going to do now? Where could I go? Inside my heart I cried, "Jesus, help me. I don't know what to do!" I raised my swollen eyes toward heaven and looked for God's help.

Something made me look to my right. There stood a huge tree with branches that could provide a covering. I ran to the tree and threw my arms around its trunk. I pressed the side of my face into its bark as if it were the softest pillow. I sobbed and hugged the tree.

Soon, a kind, small voice spoke and quieted my despair. The voice said, "It's okay. Go home now." Immediately, I felt peace soothe my heart and mind. I released the tree and headed toward my parents' place. As I neared the wire fence surrounding the projects, I saw my mother's silhouette positioned in my path. I began to walk past her and she spewed, "Where have you been? Get home right now!"

I knew that God had spoken to me as I pressed my face into the tree's bark. He gave me the peace and strength to continue on during my most desperate night alone. Some forty years later, this experience would emerge again and comfort me through a time of excruciating pain.

Chapter Six
SHATTERED DREAM

Yea, though I walk through the valley of the shadow of death, I will fear no evil; for You are with me.
Psalm 23:4 (NKJV)

By the time I finished sixth grade, some major things had changed at home. My father was home in the evenings more, and my parents had adopted their second child, a son. But still the feelings of defectiveness, anxiety, and fear ruled the way I saw myself and saw the world around me.

One day after school, my father met me at the door. This was very unusual; he was never home before I was.

"Do you remember my younger sister who lives in LA?" he asked. I felt a growing uneasiness.

"Yes, of course," I said softy. How could I ever forget my father's pretty, happy sister from the few times I had seen her when I was a little girl. He was talking about my real mom! She was going to rescue me—at least this was the dream that kept me going.

"She died," he said, with a dark and sad face.

My biological mother was dead. Her boyfriend had murdered her and her unborn baby. No one in my family had ever spoken out loud of the fact that she was my birth mother; the secret was known but hidden, as all family secrets are.

When I heard that my birth mom had died, a vivid memory of her crystallized in my mind from when I was around four years old. She had come to my parents' apartment to take me somewhere in downtown LA. She held my hand. We went for a walk. She introduced me to a man, a very tall man, the tallest man I had ever seen. They turned their faces downward toward me. My head tilted back to look up into their smiling faces. Her eyes were soft and kind. I wore a pretty pink dress and shiny black patent leather shoes. The pretty lady held my hand and was nice to me. For those few moments, I felt special. That was the happiest day of my little girl life.

And now she was dead. My childhood dream that she would one day return to rescue me and take me home with her was shattered.

That night, at age eleven, I tried to commit suicide for the first time in my life (but not the last) by overdosing on my mother's sleeping pills. As I was slipping into blurry unconsciousness, one thought formed in my benumbed mind. "God, please *help me*." And then, blackness.

My dad's hand vigorously shaking my shoulder roused me from my drugged stupor. "Someone's here. Get up!" he firmly whispered with his face close to mine. A woman who knew my mom appeared at our door that night. It was the only time a friend of my parents ever dropped by unannounced. It was a miracle that I survived that evening.

Chapter Seven
Self-Protection

I cry out loudly to God,
loudly I plead with God for mercy.
Psalm 142:1 (MSG)

God had other plans for the desperate eleven-year-old girl I had become. I never told anyone what I had done—what I had almost done—the night I learned of my birth mother's violent death.

But my depression grew as my feelings of loss, unworthiness, and shame deepened during my adolescence.

At age fourteen, my childhood physical abuse ceased. My mom was only five feet two inches tall. I had surpassed her height by six inches somewhere around my twelfth birthday. But she continued her regular demeaning and often physically painful assaults well into my adolescence.

One momentous summer day, my mom was raging at me and spitting out familiar degrading and shaming epithets. We stood face to face in the kitchen, and, within seconds of her spewing her verbal abuse my way, she positioned herself to launch a physical assault. Just inches from my body, she grabbed her ten-gallon weighted purse, raised it over her head, and aimed it at my face.

But for the first time in my thirteen-plus years of physical and emotional abuse, I raised my hand and stopped her weapon mid-air. Her face contorted into a look of shock and disbelief. I screamed, "You'll never, ever hit me again!"

In that moment, years of fear and vulnerability exploded in the newly opened space in my mind. I had escaped a vicious assault. I had triumphed over the shadow monster!

With heart pounding, I ran out of the house, crying but feeling liberated from physical tyranny. I raced across the street and dashed up the numerous stairs leading to a Catholic church at the top of the hill. Still shaken, I sat on a stone by the massive oak door, hugging my knees to my chest. My tears flowed, and I quickly brushed them away. I cried, prayed, and watched the thunderclouds gather in the northeastern skyline. I felt something I identified as freedom.

But underneath it all, like a solid layer of impenetrable rock, I also felt wickedness—like I still was, in truth, a bad, bad girl. The message that "God doesn't help bad little girls" still had root in my soul. Even though I had finally stopped the one I thought of as "the shadow monster," I didn't feel at all good about myself.

What kind of person would have to fight against her own mom, I thought. How bad must I be that my biological mother didn't want me and my adoptive mom despised me?

And then there was that ultimate rejection—God didn't help me escape such a terrible home, such awful, ongoing abuse. I had no one to rely on, no one to help me. No, even though I had felt a fleeting moment of triumph, I still felt numb, sad, isolated, abnormal, and depressed.

I remained on the church steps for about two hours, trying to compose myself, considering my options. Eventually, I headed back home aware that, fundamentally, nothing had changed.

After I returned home that night, I began to dabble with my mother's prescription diet pills and sleeping pills. They altered my feelings, and I liked feeling something other than myself, other than reality. The relief washed over my entire being, soothing and exciting me.

At thirteen and a half, I had also begun bingeing and purging occasionally—eating a lot of food, then making myself vomit, silently, so no one within hearing range would know. This process gave me a false sense of control in an environment that was so horribly unpredictable and shameful.

By age fourteen, I was growing ever more numb, rebellious, and disconnected. I felt inadequate and isolated. My mother continued to verbally abuse me, calling me names, criticizing my looks and actions, and generally berating me.

One day in high school, I nodded out during a biology lab class. I had taken a couple of my mother's sleeping pills earlier, and the effects were kicking in. A few friendly classmates crowded around my desk, roused me, and asked what was wrong. One of the students was my cousin. Even though I downplayed my sleepiness, she went home and told her mother—my aunt— that I appeared to be on drugs.

My aunt called my mother, and when I got home, my mother was hysterically angry. It had been a while since I had seen and experienced the physical manifestations of her rage. Her contorted appearance stunned me.

"What's wrong with you? Are you stupid? You're no good. No good!"

The slew of insults, degradations, and angry, vicious words poured down. I desperately wanted to leave, go to a friend's house—escape. But my mother was having none of that. "You're not going anywhere!" She still had a power over me that paralyzed me in those moments, and I didn't run away.

Word of the school sleepiness episode traveled fast. That same evening, a different cousin of mine called and asked, "Can you come with me to church? There's a special speaker tonight." She said a man who had been imprisoned at San Quentin would be presenting. He was a former heroin addict whose life had been changed by God. Now he was an evangelist for Jesus Christ.

That invitation sounded intriguing—plus, going with my cousin would get me out of the house for a few hours. The only reason my mother let me go was that the event was being held at a church.

I was definitely ready to hear a message of hope and change. After listening to the ex-con whose once-wretched life had been turned to one of tranquility, I recommitted my teenage life to Jesus Christ and was baptized in the Holy Spirit and received my prayer language that night.

Filled with God's power and love, I became a "holy roller" and "on fire" for Jesus. I was reminded of the peace I had felt as a young child in Bible school, contemplating the beautiful painting of the river flowing into eternity. For the first time in my adolescent life, I felt joy, security, and something close to peace.

Unfortunately, as fate would have it, these feelings didn't last for very long. But many years later, the touch of the Holy Spirit's fire I felt that night saved me from a certain death.

Chapter Eight
THE RUNAWAY

Wait for the Lord, and he will make things right.
Proverbs 20:22 (NCV)

I'm thankful that I did experience some happy moments in my childhood and adolescence, at school, at church, and playing outdoors solo or with friends. The church opened up an escape path for me—physical escape and emotional escape from the painful abuse I had come to accept as inevitable, as normal.

The emotions I felt in the new church I attended as a teenager reminded me of how I felt when, as a young child, I would look at the river picture and dream I could step into it and know peace. The Baptist church of my childhood had provided the hope of escape—escape into the loving arms of the Lord. Now as a teenager, I was committing myself to my relationship to Christ. I felt free.

And then, at age eighteen, I managed a physical escape. I moved out of my parents' house immediately upon my eighteenth birthday and moved in with a godly woman from my church. A well-respected woman of our church, she had opened her home to teenaged girls like me who needed a place to live. But my act of independence didn't leave behind feelings of despair and anger. My emotional wounds were branded into my spirit, soul, and body. Instead of projecting my pain and anger onto others, I turned it inward. Thus began a very dark period in my young adult life.

It didn't take long for me to find another, more exciting escape route. A short time after I left home, I married a twenty-one-year-old young man who had traveled from Brooklyn, New York, evading a warrant for his arrest. My soon-to-be husband settled in my rural town, accepted Christ into his heart, and began performing with my church's music ministry.

Right from the start, he was attracted to me. Several weeks later, he asked me to marry him and, to please the pastor, I said yes. Marriage was expected among the youth of our church; premarital sex was strictly forbidden. All of my friends had married by the time our pastor encouraged my boyfriend and me to wed. It was the thing to do, even if it wasn't the right thing; sex outside of the bond of marriage was a grave sin. And so, even though I didn't have a clue about what love was, or who my boyfriend really was, and even though I had known him for barely six months, I agreed to marry him.

Immediately following our one-night honeymoon, my husband and I started to have issues. His main interest was playing guitar and having sex. And he had no desire or ability to be a loving and kind partner in bed. I was a virgin on our wedding night. Consummating our marriage was very difficult and painful. The pain never lessened with time. I had no one to talk to about this depressing problem, so I turned to the pastor for a solution. That was a big mistake.

In his small, stuffy office in the back of the church, the pastor told me that I had to "do what your husband says. You're under his authority now." In my mind, these words diminished my value to this pastor, the church, and God.

I felt worthless once again, and my heart was hurting. With dread and a sense of dejection, I returned home to my husband.

In the summer of 1973, we moved to Brooklyn, where my husband's family still lived. We left the pastor and his church. And we left behind my family and friends—pretty much every connection I had ever made in my life.

When we arrived in Brooklyn, my husband's family threw a reception for us. I took my first drink of alcohol there. I was only eighteen.

In August 1974, I became pregnant with my first child. My husband took a job in Manhattan, and we rented a three-room apartment above a pizza parlor in Brooklyn. We lived within a block of the above-ground F train. The intermittent noise from the train was a constant reminder of my isolation during the long days when my husband was gone. He was gone at least five or six days out of the week. He worked all the time plus overtime. It seemed like his company never closed. I remained alone in the apartment with no social life.

Eventually, I learned that my husband, the middle child of an alcoholic father, had begun using heroin—again. On the rare days he did not work, my husband would take his guitar and go out, leaving me alone in our tiny, bare-bones apartment. I had no car, no family, no prenatal care, and no money. My husband had become my world. Sadly for us both, we did not place the Lord Jesus at the center of our marriage. This self-centered and unspoken decision would cost us our marriage.

My husband's family knew he used drugs, but no one had ever told me about it. Apparently, his brother had been using hard drugs for quite some time too. I remained in the dark about my husband's habit for several months, unaware that I was living with an active addict and clueless about what that actually meant.

About seven months into my pregnancy, I spotted a bent hypodermic needle in our bathroom. I confronted my husband. True to addict form, he denied knowing anything about it. But his denial was unconvincing. Even though I was capable of being fooled about many things, this time, I trusted my gut.

Acting on my hunch, after he went out one evening, I took the train to the stop that was closest to his brother's apartment. I exited the train and walked across the elevated platform. From the right vantage point, I could get a view of his brother's apartment. I was desperately hoping that our car wasn't there, that my husband was somewhere other than his brother's drug pit, that my suspicions about his drug addiction were unfounded.

But as I reached the end of the train platform and looked across the street, I could see our car parked right in front of the apartment. Rage flared. My stomach knotted. Deflated and shaken, I turned around and stumbled back on the train. By the time I returned to our apartment, a life-altering change had begun.

Right then, I made a decision. I left him in Brooklyn and returned to the Southwest, but not just because he was using drugs. I had no prenatal care in Brooklyn. And I was hungry.

Reluctantly, I returned to my parents' home. I immediately arranged to get prenatal care through the Indian Health Services. I was nearly eight months pregnant when I finally saw an obstetrician.

It was so depressing to live again in my parents' home. The tension, shame, and repressed anger in that household made for an extremely uncomfortable living situation, but it was better than toughing it out with an active heroin abuser.

A few weeks after I moved home, my beautiful baby girl was born in the local hospital. My husband wasn't there for her birth, nor did he help take care of her during the most difficult time— when I brought this tiny infant home to my parents' house. I was a nineteen-year-old mother living in the home of my childhood abuser. Feelings of shame and guilt welled up whenever I thought about my situation—married to a heroin user who had all but abandoned his baby girl and me.

Through this dark season of leaving my husband and rejoining my parents, I continually prayed for my Heavenly Father's help. Although I didn't understand why my life was so messed up, I did know that God was somewhere watching me.

My husband had a change of heart shortly after the baby arrived. He came back to be with us two weeks after she was born. He said he had sworn off drugs for good; he wanted to be a family.

But ultimately, his limited skills proved inadequate. He gave up on finding a job and he returned to Brooklyn … and to heroin.

Chapter Nine
ADDICTED

There is now no condemnation
for those who are in Christ Jesus.
Romans 8:1 (NIV)

My life may have been better if the baby and I had remained separated from my husband. Shortly before our baby girl turned one year old, I returned to Brooklyn to visit my husband and his parents and brothers. They had never met our daughter.

Even though I loved my baby beyond measure, I was exhausted. I felt ages older than my nineteen years.

One fall night in Brooklyn, my husband and I went over to his brother's house. I saw my husband, his brother, and his brother's common-law wife go into a bathroom then emerge with a different attitude and aura among them. They exhibited a camaraderie that increased my sense of separateness. They were experiencing something to-gether that seemed to draw them closer. I was the only one not joining in.

I felt odd—like an outsider, and I desperately wanted to belong. I watched them from the sofa as they sat at the kitchen table nodding and talk-ing in unfamiliar tones. My husband's brother goaded me, "I've got something that'll make you feel much better. Don't be so shy. Join us."

Out of my desperate need to belong, I made the tragic choice to join them. I nodded my head in agreement and my husband came over to me, placed my hand under his arm, tied a belt around my bicep, slapped the soft part of my inner arm, and popped the needle into my most prominent vein. Within seconds my innocence evaporated. I experienced the indescribable high of heroin for the first time.

From that first heroin use, my husband continued to "get me off," and I didn't object. We now had something in common. For me it was a way to feel peace, or just to escape the reality of my life and who I had become. I could not have fathomed that

I would ever be so stupid or so low as to try heroin—much less allow anyone to stick me with a needle.

But by the time I was twenty-three years old, I was fully addicted to this incredibly powerful drug. It is only by the grace of God that I am alive to share this story with you.

It's hard to describe the intensity of this addiction to someone who has no firsthand experience with the physical, mental, and emotional terrors an addict faces when no drugs are within easy reach. It's one thing to have to go for a day without a smartphone, or to miss an episode of a favorite TV show, or even to go without coffee for a week. Those things can be easily replaced, and no serious or long-term physical, mental, or emotional symptoms occur when stopping the "addiction."

And unlike the caffeine addict, whose withdrawal symptoms may include a day or two of headaches, the heroin addict—or any other opioid addict—becomes willing to take desperate measures if faced with a supply cut-off. By "desperate measures" I mean searching the streets for dealers whose product could contain deadly doses of other dangerous drugs; abandoning children, spouses, friends, and jobs in the quest to use again; and making drug buys, knowing that the seller could turn out to be an undercover officer and the transaction could mean a future behind bars.

None of those consequences will deter an opioid addict from trying to obtain the next dose. People who are addicted and facing withdrawal—whether voluntary or involuntary withdrawal—are lost souls. They can't think straight. They freak out over pretty much anything, and their actions often result in harm to themselves or other people.

I know, because I walked this godforsaken path, and not just once. What I experienced was horrible.

Chapter Ten
Sexual Assault

I sought the Lord, and he answered me; he delivered me from all my fears. Those who look to him are radiant; their faces are never covered with shame.
Psalm 34:4—5 (NIV)

At twenty-three years of age, I was a young mother in an abusive marriage to a heroin addict. And I was also a heroin abuser. I had been raped by two different men, one of them my husband's brother. Looking back on it, that painful fact seems far more terrible than it did at the time. Familiar feelings of shame, guilt, and confusion wash over me when my thoughts devolve into the awful feeling that I somehow deserved this treatment.

One of the rapes resulted in a pregnancy, which my doctor recommended I terminate due to the high risk of infant abnormalities associated with the medications prescribed to me after the rape. It was a decision I lived to regret and carried deep remorse over. My memory of that time period is dim; I was like a sleepwalker or zombie. Nonetheless, I continued to live with my husband and raised our daughter in a home where drug use was commonplace.

In the fall of 1977, I caught sight of our three-year-old little girl mimicking mommy and daddy by looping a leather belt around her upper arm like a tourniquet. I froze.

"Dear God, what am I doing?" I thought, choking back tears.

That grotesque sight did it for me. In a flash, my path became crystal clear. I fell to my knees and cried out to the Lord, "Oh God, help me for I have greatly sinned and I need your forgiveness, your help. Lead my daughter and me to safety. Help me, Father!"

God heard my cry and made a way out. Within twenty-four hours, I left my husband, took our daughter back to my parents' home, and never looked back.

We divorced in the early 1980s. My husband had minimal contact with our daughter during her childhood, a painful situation for her to bear. He died in 2006 of cirrhosis of the liver. I was told his liver ruptured and he bled out in his room one night while playing his guitar. Music was one of his greatest gifts.

His brother, a heroin abuser who often shared his needles when getting me high, had died during the first wave of AIDS deaths in 1985.

I was able to quit heroin with no symptoms of withdrawal—a miracle, some would say. Maybe my mothering instinct was stronger than the heroin addiction at that time. What I do know is that the Lord intervened in our lives. I prayed for help, confessed my sins, and asked my heavenly Father for forgiveness and a way out. I walked the path God showed me to escape.

There is no question that God delivered me from heroin. I have learned that He delights to work through our lives in powerful ways, but our sin keeps us from experiencing His fullness. As I walked in close relationship to the Lord, my heroin use was behind me. The drug-addiction chapter of my life was over … at least for the time being.

Soon I was able to apply and get admitted to college.

Chapter Eleven
ECSTASY AND AGONY

You can go to God Most High to hide.
You can go to God All-Powerful for protection.
Psalm 91:1 (ERV)

God mercifully freed me from heroin abuse when I courageously left my addicted husband. Abandoning one's spouse was considered a shameful act in Native culture. My dad was strong in this belief. Even though I had a great reason for leaving him, I wouldn't tell my parents. My dad would despise my husband and, even worse, he would be so disappointed in me. I couldn't bear to reveal my tale of marital heroin abuse. Yuck!

I was disgusted with myself. I believed only the lowest of society injected heroin. I never imagined that I would allow a needle to pierce my skin unless it was a vaccination. I felt shameful, isolated, and guilty. Adding to my shame was the fact that I removed my daughter from her dad. So I foolishly thought that our heroin abuse needed to remain a secret. My shame kept me silent. I chose their disapproving eyes and silent judgments while I figured out my next steps.

How was I going to take care of my toddler? I had a high school degree and one semester of Bible school. Could I get a job in Bible studies? I knew how to find the sixty-six books of the Bible, but who would pay me for this "talent"? Darn! Truly, I didn't have any marketable skills. I was just another statistic—an unskilled, unemployed, single young mother.

Yet, I was determined to improve our lives. I wasn't going to let my feeling loss or shame stop me. College was the answer to my daughter's security and better life opportunities. The only way out of my poverty was a college education. I trusted God and stepped forward.

While living with my parents, I got a full-time job, saved money, and applied for college financial aid through our tribal higher education office. I completed stacks of paperwork for college admittance, scholarships, loans, and grants. It was tedious but necessary. My hard work paid off. Due to financial aid and savings, I paid for family housing, bus passes, childcare, registration, books, and supplies. Financial aid was limited, so my daughter and I qualified for food stamps. Hopeful and nervous, I took my daughter and we moved to the college town. Less than a year after leaving heroin behind, I was headed to the state university.

I excelled in college. Undergraduate studies required attendance and participation in class. Consistently engaging in classes allowed me to ace my tests. I felt approval and competent. When my absences from classes resulted in lower test scores, I felt distress and disappointment. I vividly recall that, early in my undergraduate career, I ditched most of my US History classes. The topic simply didn't hold my interest. I preferred skipping this class for drinking margaritas, chowing on Buffalo wings, and bingeing on video games. Unfortunately, my leisure choices brought negative results; my history grade was a C—tragic! How could this be? I was an A student. Something had to change because an average grade was unacceptable! So I changed my behavior from "absent and partying" to "present and attentive."

My determination paid off. I graduated with academic distinction. Magna cum laude was embossed on my bachelor's degree in elementary education. Wow! What a powerful academic recognition. This was another example of God's favor in my life. It was a good confirmation of my God-given intellectual talent. This academic achievement propelled me like a rocket from Cape Canaveral.

I loved going to college. It suited me, and I thrived on meeting the challenges of new assignments, stretching my skills and knowledge. I graduated four years after I was admitted to college. I was twenty-seven.

Chapter Twelve
Harvard Journey

Let's keep focused on that goal,
those of us who want everything God has for us.
Philippians 3:15 (MSG)

After one year of teaching in an untraditional third grade classroom, I interviewed for a position teaching gifted students in the district's Accelerated Learning Program School (ALPS). This acclaimed school was the state's largest gifted program for inner city students. The competition for this rare position was keen. Although a novice teacher, I was chosen from a pool of thirty experienced teachers to join this unique teaching team. God's favor, combined with my experience, academic record, and enthusiasm, set me apart from the other applicants. When the ALPS director, who became my co-teacher and lifetime mentor, offered me this position, I was ecstatic.

I bloomed like a springtime wildflower in this creative teaching environment. We nurtured a culture of acceptance and excellence. Our students buzzed with excitement as they explored new ideas and processes for sharing information. We designed research assignments that accentuated our student's intellectual strengths, stimulated their higher thinking skills, and promoted positive self-images. I felt proud of my role in our students' accomplishments, and yet, I felt incomplete. My students' learning experiences ignited my passion for achievement and fueled my curiosity. I wanted to learn more. I made the decision to apply to graduate school for my master's degree.

Classrooms throughout my elementary and high school years were safe harbors. My esteem came from my teachers' accolades for being an attentive, well-behaved student and a quick thinker. I excelled academically. School was a silo in my life that didn't draw my mother's abuse. God couldn't control her rage, but He created me with a keen intellect and charismatic personality. I easily made friends in school, loved to make them laugh, and enjoyed taking tests.

Before I was ten, God planted a seed in my heart about an important school I heard about called Harvard. It was crystal clear that I was going to Harvard. What a delightful and bright student I was! My consistent positive school experiences set the stage for my success in higher education.

Harvard University is designed for the brightest students in the world. Motivated by excitement and confidence, I eagerly tackled the intense graduate college application process. I never doubted that I would make it to Harvard. When my acceptance letter arrived, it confirmed God's plan for the next step in my life's journey.

The greatest challenge to attending Harvard was my daughter. By the mid-eighties, her father and I were divorced. He had since remarried, had other children, and had limited involvement with my daughter. My little girl would be entering fifth grade and she had a serious health condition. She struggled with allergies and asthma attacks. She took more daily medications then I had kitchen spices. Winter's thin air didn't treat her kindly. Cold seemed to trigger the most extreme struggles to breathe. I couldn't justify subjecting her to the east coast's bitterly cold winter. How was I going to attend Harvard and still care for my daughter? Again, God had a plan and opened a door.

My parents were the solution. They told me she could live with them for the few months that I was at Harvard. "It's no problem; we'd love to have her. It's too far to take her and there's a school just a couple of blocks away." It seemed like a good option, although I felt uneasy about leaving her behind. I wasn't concerned about any abuse issues; my mother never raged against my daughter. Rather I was concerned about being separated for nine months. We had never been apart for that long. My daughter's well-being was my first priority, so I accepted my parents' offer.

I was excited to start my adventure, and departure day finally arrived. My heart raced as the plane lifted. I mentally checked off all my to-dos required for this two-thousand-mile journey. My large trunk was shipped earlier in the week so that my belongings would be awaiting my arrival. Yes, everything was checked off on my list. I leaned back, prayed, and relaxed.

Almost five hours later, my plane descended on a rainy night into Boston's airport. Raindrop streams formed on my window as my eyes strained to see the silhouetted skyscrapers bordering the runway. I softly spoke, "We made it Lord. I'm here."

With luggage in hand, I jumped into the nearest cab and confidently said, "84 Brattle St, Cambridge, please." My nose nearly touched the backseat window as the cab chauffeured to me though the wet, shiny streets of Boston, across the Charleston River, and stopped in front of a cobbled sidewalk. The low glow of the streetlights illuminated the sidewalk in front of my new home, the Cronkite Graduate School dorm. Clearly, it was an impressive building to match the notable address. I paid the cab driver and he quickly sped away. I stood there by my luggage, taking in the most noble structure before me. As if it were plucked from the pages in children's book, this charming, three-story, reddish-brick building, adorned with white framed windows, was my new home. What a great first impression! I felt relieved.

My hand grasped the white-paneled door and turned the brass doorknob. When I entered lobby, there were two welcoming young faces behind the reception counter. Several mailboxes were behind the counter and I figured my large trunk was nearby. I glanced around but it was out of my eyesight. After proper greetings were exchanged, I was handed my keys and directed upstairs. I asked for my trunk. My body began to heat up as a young man shook his head and said, "Sorry, it's not here." With rising concern, I asked again for my trunk. The student said, "Nope, we haven't received anything," as he looked behind him just to confirm what he already believed.

My heart dropped. Excited feelings about Harvard were replaced by fear and loneliness.

"What! No, trunk! No personal bedding, towels, and belongings?" I quietly exclaimed. My confident stance was fading fast. I wanted to go home.

"Are you sure it's not here? Please check again." I hoped that my worn leather trunk would serendipitously appear beneath the parcel piles. Alas, my trunk was not there. The items I had packed were crucial to helping me adjust to this distant place. It included many dear pictures. But most of all, I had packed a tiny Bible inscribed with a personal message from my father. Distress weighted my brow as I thanked the assistants, picked up my suitcases, and turned toward the stairs.

One of the young men offered to help me with my luggage. I gratefully accepted. I couldn't bear walking to my room by myself. The beauty of this dorm with its antiqued architecture, brick walls, and wooden staircases was muted by my despair. My loneliness was growing and almost suffocating. I prayed, "God help me. I want to go home."

My dorm room was no bigger than a small walk-in closet. A miniature, old-time desk with a chair was next to the twin-sized bed. One window with faded curtains was opposite of the door we entered. The room matched my feeling of isolation.

I felt desperate. Holding back the tears, I thanked the young man. As the door closed behind him, I exhaustedly plopped down on the uncovered mattress. Tears slid down my cheeks. Where was God now? Why did God bring me all the way here to feel more alone? I prayed and cried and then decided to call my best friend who had helped me pack, driven me to the airport, and watched my plane depart. We didn't have cell phones, so I went downstairs and used the pay phone.

Crying over a lost trunk may seem extreme. However, I was a stranger in Massachusetts. I was alone and feeling insecure. I believed that my belongings would've helped me to fit in so far away from home. I didn't want to feel like a stranger. I wanted to belong. My anxiety increased and I reached out for help.

Once on the phone with my friend, she exclaimed, "Did you get there okay? I'm so glad you called!" My sobs caught her attention. With a changed tone, she asked, "What's wrong?"

I spoke between sobs, "Help me! My trunk didn't get here. I don't have any of my belongings. I want to go home."

Her compassionate words flowed through the phone line and soothed my distress. Her words kept me from leaving, "I'll catch the next flight out and help you. We'll take care of what you need. Just hold tight."

This experience was a pivotal point in my journey. A friend's helping hand kept me on the best path. God knew exactly what I needed to prevent me from missing this opportunity. He arranged the circumstances in my friend's life so that she help me in a critical time. She responded sacrificially using her time and money. If she hadn't offered to come, I would have given up, overwhelmed by the enormity of my decision to leave everything behind. But God made a way and I stayed. My trunk eventually showed up.

A second pivotal experience occurred the day after my arrival. Harvard's main campus was a five-minute walk from my dorm. It was a clear August day when I headed to explore the campus. As soon as I stepped through the wrought-iron gate onto Harvard Yard's expansive, grass-covered lawn, I was awestruck. I had entered into a green canopied oasis inside an urban jungle. Flowering trees, red-brick buildings, cobble-stone pathways, and bustling students filled this enclave. The famous John Harvard sculpture was prominently positioned in the Yard.

Suddenly, the imposter syndrome hit. Here I was standing on the lawn of the world's most prestigious university. I was starting a master's degree program at Harvard Graduate School of Education. Surely someone was going to figure out the admissions committee made a mistake. I panicked. "Oh no, I'm not smart enough to be here. What was I thinking?" As quickly as these self-defeating thoughts attacked, I replaced them with prayer. Leaning against the bark of a tree, I raised my eyes toward the sky. My pounding heart calmed as I prayed, "God, thank you for leading me here. Your Word says your plans for me are good. I believe you. Let's look around!" From that time on, I replaced negative thoughts about my school worthiness with positive self-talk. "I can do this! God's for me!" I determined to do whatever necessary to succeed.

Once classes started, I was positioned alongside the most brilliant and accomplished professors and graduate students. My adjustment to East

Coast culture and this prestigious institution was easier than expected. I acclimated to my new life with a determined attitude and an active pursuit of resources. I reached out for support from staff, students, and other college programs both on and off campus to understand how they could help me succeed. I eagerly took advantage of their help.

Inserting myself into the diverse student communities at Harvard greatly helped me feel connected. I served as the president of the American Indian Graduate Students Association at Harvard. This group was a great source of community and support. Like me, my fellow Native students also left their communities to attend this college in hopes of a better future for their families, their people, and their reservations. We each needed to feel a sense of community living so far from home. As president, I organized relationship-building opportunities and social activities. This was my first elected office and it released God-given leadership qualities. I felt accepted and valued when helping other students feel supported.

Two Indigenous mentors and one course were significant in my Harvard experience and my path to law school. A Jewish professor taught the most exciting class, The Law and Higher Education.

This professor was a former civil rights attorney and educator with both a law degree and an education doctorate degree from Harvard. His achievements, teaching style, and legal mind expanded my thinking about career opportunities. He promoted intellectual curiosity and challenged my assumptions about societies and Indigenous justice. This class was also designed for the elite Harvard law students. These classmates were enrolled in our nation's top ranked law school and I was impressed. We engaged in fascinating intellectual readings and class discussions that expanded the corners of my thinking. Unbeknownst to me, this course would become my training ground for the study of law. But God knew.

The second mentor was my Harvard boyfriend. The first time I laid eyes on this dark-haired, mustached man, I was standing in our dorm's reception area. I overheard him ask the dorm attendant a bizarre question, "Where's the nearest golf course?" Puzzled by his question, I began sizing him up. Wearing a fashionable beige trench coat with a red woolen scarf, this man looked like Cambridge gentry. And, interestingly, I thought that he looked Mexican. Such a question seemed very odd coming from a Mexican man. I had never heard of a Mexican American or an American Indian golfer. Nonetheless, this handsome Mexican-looking gentleman was interested in golfing and I was interested in him.

Soon this Hispanic golfer became my boyfriend and trusted mentor. He had great listening skills and we quickly discovered that we shared many similar values about God, justice, identity, and community. Woven throughout our conversations was his passion for law. Enrolled in Harvard's Kennedy School of Government, he was a practicing attorney from the Southwest and was thrilled to be a graduate student studying public policy. After graduation, he'd return home with a Harvard degree and make an even greater community contribution. His professional approach to learning and experiencing all that Harvard had to offer was contagious. Together we embraced once-in-a-lifetime encounters with international dignitaries, intellectual powerhouses, and nationally recognized political figures such as anti-apartheid and human rights activist Bishop Desmond Tutu; Sally Ride, the first US woman astronaut; and the Kennedys—Ethel, John Jr., Caroline, Ted, and Michael. My boyfriend's admiration for my intellect was humbling and uplifting. Through his eyes and mentorship, I saw my potential as a powerful influencer competent to follow in his legal footsteps.

God's hand in orchestrating my journey from Harvard to law school is undeniable. My faith, mentors, graduate studies, intellectual curiosity, and sense of obligation to serve my tribe all factored into inspiring me to study the law and expand my leadership skills.

Graduation day arrived and Harvard buzzed with excited students, proud families, and prestigious faculty. Large clusters of white folding chairs were scattered across the campus's freshly manicured lawns. My mother and daughter flew in to attend my graduation and I felt relieved. Yet I also felt deep sadness that my father didn't come.

By graduation day, I had successfully completed the grueling Law School Admissions Test (LSAT), sent applications to six nationally ranked law schools, and received five acceptance letters. I decided to attend a top-ten law school that sent me a brochure boasting of its sizable number of American Indian law students. Excited about joining this law school's Native law students' community, I decided to attend UC Berkeley's School of Law, one of the premier law schools in the United States.

Chapter Thirteen
BERKELEY LAW

Wise people treasure knowledge.
Proverbs 10:14 (NLT)

Shortly after Harvard graduation, I returned home to my daughter. I spent the summer tutoring elementary aged children on my reservation. When the summer ended, I bought a sturdy ten-year-old station wagon, packed our humble belongings, and hit the highway to our future in Berkeley, California. Together we left family, friends, and community behind in search of a better opportunity for ourselves and for my tribal community. I reasoned that if I was "smart" enough to study the law, then I had an obligation to my tribe to earn a law degree and use it for their good. I knew God was with us and that attending law school was part of His plan for our future.

As we arrived in Berkeley, the magnificent Bay Bridge rose from behind Berkeley's family housing property and stretched across the bay to San Francisco's shoreline. Cool ocean-like air accompanied the luscious green landscape surrounding our aged, former military barracks, housing complex. Moving our car slowly through this unfamiliar property, we eventually located our barrack building and landed an upstairs apartment. Settling into family housing and settling my daughter into a nearby middle school went smoothly. This was our home for the next three years of law school.

Entering Berkeley Law as a first-year law student was a great accomplishment. Most of my classmates descended from a long line of legally trained minds—from legal scholars, to attorneys, to federal court judges. I felt intimidated and ill-prepared in spite of my Harvard background. I was the first person from my tribe to attend law school. My ancestors had fought to survive the ravages of American laws on their identity and their homelands; they didn't have access to legal education. I also felt privileged and a sense of pride because I had a seat in this distinguished institution. The administration regularly reminded us that we were the *crème de la crème* of law students across the country and that getting into this top-ten law school was the hardest part. For me, the hardest part was the first year of law school. God blessed me with two Indigenous women mentors who helped me make it through the grueling academic year.

One trusted mentor was Monica. She introduced herself on my first day of law school and we quickly learned that we were assigned to the same contracts class. She was as personable as she was petite. With thick wavy black hair, sparkling eyes, and an endless reserve of hugs, this was a woman who never met a stranger. We instantly became close friends and study partners. Our values about justice, community, and identity were similar.

Born of immigrant parents from Mexico, Monica was a mighty advocate for social justice and determined to help the under-represented get access to legal resources. She understood the value of a seat at the table. She stood up against a biased and misappropriated use of academic policy to remove her from a legal education. Monica displayed great courage and determination to remain in law school against all odds. She fought for her opportunity to learn the law because she knew that it led to a bigger purpose. Monica graduated with her juris doctorate, passed the California bar, and returned to her community as a licensed criminal attorney. Her resiliency and commitment to learn helped increase my fortitude when I faced seemingly insurmountable challenges.

With a keen wit and eloquent vocabulary, Brigitte was my second Indigenous mentor. A skilled debater, she was a second-year law student and a single mother. She had the poise and beauty of first lady Jacquelyn Kennedy and the grit of freedom fighter Harriet Tubman. When she talked about her heritage as a Chicana and Apache woman, her dark eyes flashed and her olive-toned face glowed with pride. She was impressively articulate with a gift for inspiring others to rise above the injustices of their circumstance.

Brigitte had a zeal for fighting injustices and voicing the needs of disenfranchised Indigenous peoples. She had an amazing analytical mind that allowed her to glide through the case law and legal writing. Her legal education became a stepping-stone for her rise to an esteemed, elected position overseeing a metropolitan city's multimillion-dollar educational system. Her mentorship helped me further my commitment to prosperity for my tribal community and other tribal nations.

But the pressures of committing to law school brought dire collateral damages. I tried my best to simultaneously manage the demands of my curriculum, an unhealthy romantic relationship, and to raise my only child. Sadly, I failed miserably in parenting and romance. I allowed the chaos of an emotionally and physically abusive relationship to spill over into my daughter's life. And she witnessed some of these abusive behaviors in our small apartment.

My daughter was twelve years old and attended a nearby middle school. It was during my final semester of law school that my little girl took an overdose of her medication. My world fell apart and I despised myself for not seeing this "cry for help" sooner.

The weeks that followed my daughter's hospitalization and recovery were dark and desperate. She was resistant to help and seemed to transform overnight from a sweet-hearted little girl into an angry, rebellious teenager—a stranger. My heart broke to see her so pained, so angry, and to know that I had let her down.

I too succumbed to the flood of despair drowning my soul. My deep depression precipitated my own attempted suicide. At one point during these dark weeks, both my daughter and I were hospitalized in different locations. I thank God for saving our lives and for carrying us both when neither of us could walk.

Medicated and under doctor's supervision for anxiety, chronic depression, and PTSD, I still attended my last semester of law school and graduated with my class. My daughter was also able to promote with her eighth-grade classmates, and we gratefully celebrated her promotion.

I knew God had given me a strong intellect and a stronger will—the will to persevere, to study, to learn all I could. I still believed that God had a purpose for me, and it involved using the mind He had blessed me with for His purposes.

Despite my deep belief in God and my escape from the horrors of heroin, I gave in to a curiosity about cocaine. My law school friends and I would sometimes go out disco dancing to escape from the stresses of books, assignments, and studying. On one occasion, while using the club's restroom, someone passed me a small vial of white powder and said, "Try this." It was a brief experience and I liked it. That was my first and only experience with cocaine during law school. Several years would pass before I ever socially used cocaine again.

Obtaining illicit drugs like cocaine was easier than one can imagine in the 1980s and 90s. Drug use flourished on college campuses and in the surrounding neighborhoods. Surprisingly, though, the drugs of the 90s resulted in fewer deaths than the deadly opioids now flooding the market two decades later.

Predictably, my social use of cocaine at private house parties and my unknowingly befriending a cocaine dealer led to my own fall into the grip of cocaine addiction. My addiction lasted for two lost years.

I started as a naïve social cocaine user for a few years, never using at my place of work or at home when my teenage daughter was there. It was usually at house parties on the weekends once or twice a month when I indulged in this party behavior.

But this drug is devious and destructive. Eventually, my mind became hooked and I felt a shift in my body as well. What was once a desire was now a need.

Reckless choices, fueled by my disease of addiction, brought horrible consequences. Yet God's hand on my life never wavered, and He spared me from death, jail, and insanity. Two desperate years were marked by overdoses and emotional breakdowns. I survived due to several brief hospitalizations for severe depressive episodes. There seemed to be no way to escape the overpowering psychological grip of cocaine. It was evil and cruelly isolating.

I fought this disease while striving to maintain a productive lifestyle and my sanity. Like many people addicted to cocaine, I strove to keep my career and addiction separate. But months of poor eating and sleeping habits began to affect me physically and mentally. Eventually, these habits did affect my ability to maintain an exceptional work ethic and be a nurturing, present parent. I deeply regret this time in my life.

I found recovery from cocaine addiction with God's help. In my desperation to overcome this disease, I committed to daily attending various

Twelve Step programs. Through these programs, I admitted my powerlessness over cocaine and surrendered my will to God.

After freedom from cocaine, I remained on a dangerous, slippery slope. Some in my social circle were still active drug users. Most addicts like getting high with others, and I chose to stay connected.

Although sober physically, my unresolved childhood trauma would fuel more harmful choices. I was in the wrong place at the right time and was offered some crystal methamphetamine. My "stinking thinking" went something like this: "No one's going to know, you're not an addict anymore, and it's only this one time." Well, this was another lie from the pit of hell. Both God and I knew what I was doing, and it would not be just one time.

Meth helped me escape. Its effects were quick and intense, and they lasted three days. So I would time my use for a Friday evening. I would go without eating or sleeping and be high for the entire weekend, hidden in my home.

During this brief meth phase, my teenage daughter was becoming a young adult. She was in high school and spent many weekends at her grandparents' home out of town. These away trips allowed me the freedom to lose myself in drug use.

My escaping wasn't as hidden as I had hoped. My teen daughter was the proverbial "lost child" in our home. My unavailability and emotional detachment brought immense instability into her life. My daughter suffered significantly from my inability to nurture and parent. She left home after her eighteenth birthday. As I think back on that time, her emotional pain was evident in many ways.

When I finally did see her pain, I stopped risking my life with meth use. I thank God that I did not become addicted to this devil's drug. But I was not out of the woods addiction-wise.

Recovery from addiction is never a straight line. The new millennium was marred by the premature death of my closest friend and the repeated, self-harming actions of an immediate family member. I was debilitated by my helplessness to ease the suffering of both my terminally ill best friend and my family member. I unknowingly entered into an unfamiliar pattern of self-control—ano-rexia.

And as my faith in God's desire to help me weak-ened, I grew more and more debilitated, physi-cally as well as emotionally. My spiritual practice waned just as my resolve to be free from addiction waned. During my late forties to early fifties, I struggled with anorexia and chronic pain. Se-verely underweight and malnourished, I entered into a Christian treatment facility for anorexic and bulimic women in January 2002.

The sixty-day-long inpatient program helped stop the steep progression of this disease. For at least five years after my release from the facility, I fought daily with the physical, mental, and emo-tional anguish of anorexia. This condition, consid-ered the most deadly of all mental health disor-ders, precipitated my disability for seven years.

The genesis of my physical pain happened in the summer of 2003. I sat in my car at a city stoplight on a clear summer evening. I waited for the light to turn green before I could proceed through the intersection. BAM! My neck jerked like a bobble head; my car had been rear-ended by a hit-and-run driver.

My injuries resulted in a doctor's referral to a pain management center. Physical therapy and pain meds were exactly what the doctor ordered.

During these times of pain and challenge, I often sensed that God was by my side. But still, I was bent on doing things my way. I believed that I had to take things into my own hands if I was going to keep from being hurt. This ungodly belief grew from the facts of my life. After all, I had evidence that even when I was an innocent little girl, God wouldn't help me, wouldn't rescue me, wouldn't strike down the shadow monster or prevent me from being abused.

By age fifty-two, I couldn't walk without a cane, in part because of pain and also due to my increased dependence on prescription medications like Oxycontin, Xanax, Oxycodone, Klonopin, Percocet, Vicodin, and Somas. At one of my doctor appointments for prescription refills, I requested a printout of the medications I was currently taking.

The list had at least fifteen different daily medications—a mixture of anti-depressants, anxiety medications, muscle relaxers, and opioids.

Finally, at age fifty-three, I hit the edge of hell, a hell worse than any I had experienced to date. Despair brought me very close to dying a physical death. But from that hell, God lifted someone precious to Him—me!

Chapter Fourteen
Deadly Detox

In their misery they cried out to the Lord,
and He saved them from their troubles.
He brought them out of their gloom and
darkness and broke their chains.
Psalm 107:13–14 (NCV)

On October 30, 2008, I undertook a forced detox. One week before that date, I had attended my regularly scheduled behavioral health appointment for prescription refills. Unfortunately, I was directed to a different psychiatrist, who was an apathetic "mini-Hitler" in bearing and attitude. I had never seen this doctor before. She possessed a frigid and unfriendly demeanor and barked out her disapproval of my prescribed high dose of a benzodiazepine (benzo), Klonopin, for my anxiety disorder. Any reduction in this medication's dosage is done gradually because an abrupt stop can lead to severe seizures and possibly death. Cruelly, this psychiatrist flat-out refused to refill my prescription.

I began to panic in her office. She nonchalantly told me, "So go to the emergency room when you feel sick." I felt scared and hopeless as I left her office. I would have dropped to my knees and begged this doctor for mercy if I had had any inkling of the nightmare that lay before me.

Within forty-eight hours, I began withdrawals while sitting in my community college art class. My stomach was cramping as I walked out and headed to my car. My pain intensified and I grew increasingly ill. Yet I drove myself three miles away to the nearest hospital emergency room.

I was hurting, alone, and quickly decomposing when I limped into the ER. Indescribable pain wracked my body because I was detoxing too rapidly from the benzos. I had left my gallon-sized bag of prescription bottles in the trunk of my car. Without my bottles, I couldn't prove what I was prescribed. Because my body and mind were in turmoil, I was unable to communicate anything other than that I needed help.

The emergency room staff had no knowledge of my long-time prescription pain and anxiety medication. In mental health lingo, I was "decompen-sating" and lacked the ability to communicate clearly. I couldn't explain my situation and I could only give them my name.

The doctor who saw me deduced that I was ad-dicted to something. She said, "We're going to send you where you can detox." The hospital kept me overnight and gave me some medication to relax. I eventually fell asleep. Very early the next morning I was driven to a nearby behavioral health center. So much time had passed, now my body was not only withdrawing from benzos, but also from my opioid pain medications.

By the time we arrived at the center, the hospital's medications were waning and the withdrawal symptoms intensifying. I managed to name my pain-management center when the center's in-take person asked. After what seemed like hours more of agonizing pain, the intake nurse was able to reach my pain doctor. He confirmed that I was an outpatient and that he had prescribed pain medications. Finally, I was given a dose of oxyco-done. I felt some relief.

During this first hellish withdrawal episode, a doctor led me into a tiny sterile office. I felt gravely ill and vulnerable. He held an opened manila file in his hands and locked his eyes on mine. He spoke about my addictions and said that he could see my pain. He guaranteed me that he could get me off both the benzos and opioids simultaneously. In my diminished mental condition, I did not question this doctor. He appeared to hold the key to my freedom from pain. So I signed the papers he handed to me and committed myself to receiving treatment immediately. I felt trusting and desperate. But as I began this detoxing process, my trust would evaporate and my desperation increase.

This doctor administered Subutex, a sublingual medication that triggered the agonizing process of a dual detox from benzos and opioids. I had thought the process would be easy, a twenty-four-hour snap. Many things—including quitting heroin—came easily to me, so why would getting off these drugs be any different? After all, I was an intelligent Harvard and law school graduate with a burning desire to eliminate any pain. How difficult could it be to medically withdraw from these narcotics simultaneously?

The answer hit me like a tsunami.

I endured an agonizing and humiliating rapid detox process in that behavioral hospital. I had sorely underestimated the power of these devastating, destructive drugs. Their roots were deeply embedded within my body, mind, and soul.

The doctor said I would be admitted into the center's detox wing for no longer than five days. He had promised me a bed in the detox wing of this facility. I felt some hope in the mounting pain. I believed that the detox nursing staff would be experienced caring for people going through medically induced withdrawals.

I quickly learned that the detox wing was full. Instead of heading there, I was led down a long hall in the behavioral wing.

There were no other physically ill people in this wing. And there was no compassion or medical help. The behavioral staff had very little tolerance for detoxing addicts. Their cold stares seemed to follow me as I was paraded past them and placed in a cold, fluorescent-lit room farthest from their station.

My stomach pain and aching intensified as I lay curled up in my bed. Waves of gut-retching nausea, dry heaves, and chills took over my body. Every nerve and muscle twisted and burned inside me. My head felt like it was about to explode.

That first night, in anguish greater than I had ever known, I rolled out of my bed, got up from the floor, and tried to find a nurse in the hall. Cramping rippled through my belly, so I held my stomach and with my other hand steadied myself along the wall. I limped up the hallway, leaned against the wall and intermittently dropped to one knee when the pain was too great. Agonizing cramps, dry heaves, fever, chills, and tremors—all the symptoms of opiate withdrawal—wracked my body and pummeled my barely functioning brain. This opiate and benzo withdrawal was gruesome. I was inching my way along the wall. The wing seemed abandoned, yet I had to get help.

Unsure if I would make it through alive, I managed to crawl to the nurse's station, crying and dry heaving. I begged the night nurse for help. At first she ignored me. But then she glanced up over her paper and compassion moved her.

"Go lie over there if you want," she said, pointing me to a thin mattress on the floor, covered in black plastic. The mattress was in the center of this tiny room behind the station; nothing else was in there. I paused. I clearly remember thinking, "I'm a prisoner, and I'm in hell." I had no choices, no relief in sight, nothing but unrelenting pain and nausea. I crawled onto the black plastic mat and curled up into the fetal position.

Everything went pitch black when I lay down. In my head, thoughts and words were racing and whirling. I was trapped in a mental firestorm of disconnected words and imagery that swept through my brain. It felt as though my brain cells were on fire. I could not slow my thinking. My brain was in chaos and I felt like surrendering to the blackness. I felt my hold on sanity slipping away. I cried "Jesus" in my mind, screamed it. "Jesus, help me!"

At some point while I tried repeating these words in my head, three supernatural experiences interrupted my mental apocalypse. First, the image of Christ in a white robe with a purple sash, with His arms outstretched, floated slowly toward me. Right away, my mind stopped racing. It focused on seeing Christ Himself, right there in front of me, three-dimensional and so close I could reach out to Him and almost touch His robe.

Second, mercifully, God kept me from insanity by thrusting into my tormented brain a billboard-sized, crystallized string of words. These powerful words, "I Can See Jesus," filled my mind and focused my thoughts. The words began to fade and God's love for me burst through in another extraordinary way.

The tree that had served as a place of refuge for me more than forty years earlier appeared in place of "I Can See Jesus." My thoughts were stilled and calm flooded my mind. As I focused on the tree, a portion of the bark lifted and floated toward me. I could both see and feel its texture on the side of my face. I was comforted, and my whole body relaxed.

God met me where I was in this time of despair, physical agony, and mental turmoil. In His unfailing love and mercy, God touched me with imagery and words that protected my sanity. Because of Him, I had survived that horrific first night of dual withdrawals. The mental wounds that resulted

from this pharmaceutical trauma would eventually
be identified and healed completely.

CHAPTER FIFTEEN
SURVIVOR

Whatever is born of God conquers the world.
1 John 5:4 (NRSV)

That first night was the beginning of four more days of withdrawals. I suffered tremendously during and after that five-day detox process.

Within a few hours of my premature release from the center, I began exhibiting bizarre behaviors at home. The first incident occurred when I vigorously sprinkled cherry-flavored Crystal Lite powder on top of leftovers before reheating them in the microwave. I thought I was shaking salt, even as I watched the red powder spread over my plate. My mistake registered when I looked at my food and everything was tinted red. Although somewhat comical—shaking red powder all over my food instead of salt—my mental skills were just beginning the steep decline.

I couldn't recall where I lived even though I was standing in my house. Anything beyond my line of vision didn't exist. I couldn't recall where my house was in relation to the nearest grocery store or even how to get there. I didn't recognize objects in my house or even what was behind a closed door. My memory was impaired in unusual ways and it took days to realize just how incapacitated I had become due to the dual detox. I was terrified of being left in my home alone because people simply disappeared if I couldn't see them.

My incapacitation continued for several months. I struggled to think or communicate clearly. I suffered episodically from amnesia, hallucinations, paranoia, and severe light sensitivity. My reflexes were stunted, my facial responses not appropriate to the situation. I was reclusive and feared noises, people, and stimuli. At some point, my daughter took me to live with her for a few weeks. She did not understand my condition and why I acted so withdrawn and insecure.

Months later, I would learn that I had suffered from a post-acute withdrawal syndrome. The behavioral center had negligently released me without a plan for my follow-up.

I almost lost my mind in that place—the wonderful mind that God had blessed me with for His purposes. Almighty God won the battle against the evil one for my soul, mind, and body. With God's help, I survived the horrific withdrawal process. My addiction to opioids and benzos was broken.

Chapter Sixteen
LOVE HEALS

"I know the plans I have for you," declares the Lord, "plans to prosper you and not to harm you, plans to give you hope and a future."
Jeremiah 29:11 (NIV)

How did my transformation come about after detox and rehab? I finally recognized that two things kept me from changing: my thinking, and the enemy's foothold in my life. I lost contact with every support person and family tie during my isolation in a series of hospitals and mental health centers following the rapid detox process.

After I returned home from my various hospital stays, I felt lost much of the time and didn't leave my home alone. But I held fast to the image of the Lord and the message of peace and hope He had delivered to me.

One day, I heard God's voice telling me to reach out to an American Indian sister in the Lord whom I had met in a Native American Bible study group years earlier. I called my friend and she invited me to an upcoming gathering of her sisters and brothers in the Lord. Their group of Native Christian singers, dancers, and prayer warriors had a name—Soaring Eagles.

This fellowship of Native and non-Native Christians embraced me with wide-open arms. Within two weeks of meeting these new friends, I was included on their mission outreach to impoverished churches and communities in Mexico. And that is when my healing—from addiction, from years of abuse, from my shame and self-loathing—truly began. I was regaining my sense of self-worth though the acceptance and love of these people of faith.

I probably seemed a bit odd at times due to the remaining acute withdrawal symptoms that were slowly diminishing. My speech was hesitant and my facial reactions in communication slow to non-existent. I struggled to regain my interpersonal communication skills. Often I felt self-conscious and robotic. Yet I kept pushing myself to interact with these friends, and I was never shunned or minimized.

Desperate to stay connected with people, I started to regularly attend a church that one of the couples in Soaring Eagles attended. This couple included me in their circle of friends. One Saturday morning, I attended a local monthly Aglow International lighthouse where the Soaring Eagles pastors were the guest speakers. The president of this Aglow group, a brilliant and loving lady, offered to mentor me on the spot. Her spiritual guidance and unconditional love proved invaluable in my journey to wellness.

My life was filled with hope, faith, and God's love. Four months after my final hospital stay in December of 2008, I was restored. God miraculously healed me of the debilitating acute withdrawal symptoms.

Chapter Seventeen
GOD'S HAND

*Trust in the Lord with all your heart and lean not
on your own understanding; in all your ways sub-
mit to him, and he will make your paths straight.*
Proverbs 3:5–6 (NIV)

Today I pursue a closer relationship with God as
my refuge, my provider, and my closest friend.
Even though I may not always understand how
God works, I know that any situation I find myself
in is no surprise to God. He will work out every
detail for my good. In His perfect timing, everything will turn out right.

Daily, I ask the Lord Jesus to show me how I am
showing up in the world, to show me my habits,
my hang-ups, and the old hurts that are holding
me back. I ask the Lord to show me my habitual
patterns of behavior and my default attitude, the
attitude that allowed the darkness and shame to
rule me.

God says that I am fearlessly and wonderfully made, and He knew me in my mother's womb. I'm so grateful for these words because growing up I didn't think anyone knew about my suffering. I didn't think anyone really knew I existed.

God never left me or turned His back on me. I understand today that God wouldn't interfere with my abusive mother's free will, but He knew that I would choose to use my free will to share how He has healed my emotional and physical wounds. He's more powerful than any circumstance, any drug, and any abuse. My love relationship with God is palpable. He has promised, "I will never leave you nor forsake you" (see Joshua 1:5; Hebrews 13:5).

As a child I suffered. My mother screamed that I was bad and unworthy of God's help. I absorbed my mother's declaration that I was "a bad girl and God doesn't help bad girls." This message penetrated my mind, will, and emotions. This message reinforced the ungodly belief that I was intrinsically flawed, that I was alone, and that I deserved the abuse. My soul was brimming with shame and desperate for an escape. In short, I was vulnerable to anything that could relieve my emotional pain.

After many decades of suffering, I submitted my mind, my thoughts, and my body to my heavenly Father. I wholeheartedly participated in individual and group therapy. Dialectical Behavioral Therapy was a life-altering therapeutic process that taught me practical coping strategies.

God's unfailing mercy and love took the mess I made of my life and turned it into a testimony of His grace. The near destruction of my life was thwarted by God's love, mercy, and grace. With the embrace and knowledge of God's love, I have been freed from old mindsets, generational curses, and PTSD that plagued me since my childhood.

Chapter Eighteen
ALL RISE

*Clothed in strength and dignity, with
nothing to fear, she smiles when she
thinks about the future.*
Proverbs 31:25 (VOICE)

My story began with the court hearing on a Native man's suicide and the resulting dispute between the grieving father and the deceased's wife. My decision was rendered that same night. I had prayed and trusted that God would reveal the right decision that would honor the competing cultural values. My faith in God's presence and the power of prayer allowed Him to bring good out of a most devastating situation. He guided my thoughts and heart to see the best answer and find peace in my decision.

I reviewed the laws. God led me to the just decision. The deceased's wife prevailed because they were still married. Based on our tribal civil laws, I had the choice to apply another jurisdiction's law when our codes were silent on the matter. I found that the wife possessed a priority claim to her husband's remains, based on her legal duty of responsibility to dispose of his remains. Therefore, she had the legal right to proceed with the Hopi burial.

A few days later, a tribal pastor who was related to the deceased's wife held a Christian memorial ceremony for the parents. I was grateful to know that his parents and siblings had their closure in the Native Christian tradition. It is always God who makes all things work for good to those who love Him.

I have no idea whether drugs played a part in the suicidal death of this young Native American man. Drug and alcohol abuse remains a serious problem for Indian communities and an epidemic in our American society. Far too many people across generational and ethnic lines lose their light, their hope, their way, due to drugs and alcohol.

God propelled my professional and personal life in ways I had never imagined. Almost a year after my last hospitalization, I interviewed for an associate judge position with my tribal nation. Humbled and excited, I accepted this important appointment the day I learned that the tribal council had selected me over six other formidable applicants. Within two years of this judicial assignment, I accepted an associate professor of law position at a law school.

In 2016 I was elected by my community to serve as a legislative member of our tribal council. It is a high honor to attain this leadership status in Indian country. For me, it is a huge privilege to give back to my community in this capacity.

As I finish this memoir, state legislatures around the country are trying to enact laws to limit the distribution of opioid drugs. But whether laws will lessen the scourge of addiction is doubtful. In my experience, something more is needed to tackle addiction, something I thankfully discovered before my earthly life was over.

I live a victorious life because my individual spirit, which I control with God's guidance, decided to pursue my destiny. I surrendered to the complex process of emotional healing from historic and family trauma.

And today, with God's help, love, and guidance, I soar! In the breath of His love, I am creating a legacy of purpose, faith, and encouragement. My heart is grateful for the abundance of joy and peace in my life. When I lay my head down to sleep, I anticipate a good rest and an exciting tomorrow morning. I am humbled by my rise into positions of influence and favor following deep despair. My passion is to mentor, guide, and encourage others to walk out God's destiny for their lives.

May you also rise up into the peace, love, and grace that God offers you!

ABOUT THE AUTHOR

Siera T. Russell is a direct descendant of the Wipukepa, a separate people of the early Yavapais from central Arizona. Her ancestors were indigenous to the Verde Valley, Oak Creek Canyon, and Boynton Canyon in Central Arizona.

Siera was first in her immediate family to graduate from college. She earned a Bachelor of Arts degree in education from Arizona State University, a Master of Arts degree in education, magna cum laude, from Harvard, and a Juris Doctorate degree from UC Berkeley's School of Law.

In 2016, Siera was elected to a three-year term as a legislative member of her tribal nation's council. Prior to this office, she was an assistant professor of law and taught Property, Criminal Procedure, Topics in Indian Law, and International Human Rights Law.

Currently, Siera presides as an associate judge for a Southwest Indian community, oversees her family's retail business, and manages Indigenous Mentors, LLC. She also serves on the Indian Bible College Board of

Trustees (Flagstaff, AZ) and on the Living Water Four-square Church Council (Cottonwood, AZ).

Siera enjoys discovering the distinctive qualities of the Verde River's parks and wildlife. She experiences the greatest joy when sharing these times with her daughter, Sacheen and granddaughter, Giovanna.

To contact Siera for virtual or in-person speaking engagements, concierge coaching, or mentoring, visit www.IndigenousMentors.com or email taketchera@gmail.com.

You Can Make a Difference

Together we can help Indigenous people and communities who struggle with addiction, violence, and suicide.

Please write a book review so that others can find this story of hope and transformation.

To write a review and share how this book has impacted you, please visit: **BIT.LY/RISINGABOVEREVIEW.**

Thank you for sharing with the world and me how God has blessed you!